Sally's beans

Story by Beverley Randell
Illustrated by Meredith Thomas

Mom went into the garden.
Sally went, too.

"Here you are, Sally,"
said Mom.
"Here are 10 beans for you."

In went the beans.

Sally looked for the beans,
day after day.

"Come up, beans," said Sally.
"Come up, beans.
Where are you?"

"My beans are up!" shouted Sally.

"Look, Mom! 1, 2, 3, 4, 5, 6, **7** beans."

Sally watered the beans,
day after day.

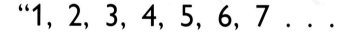

"1, 2, 3, 4, 5, 6, 7 . . .
8, 9, **10** beans!" she said.
"**Ten** beans."

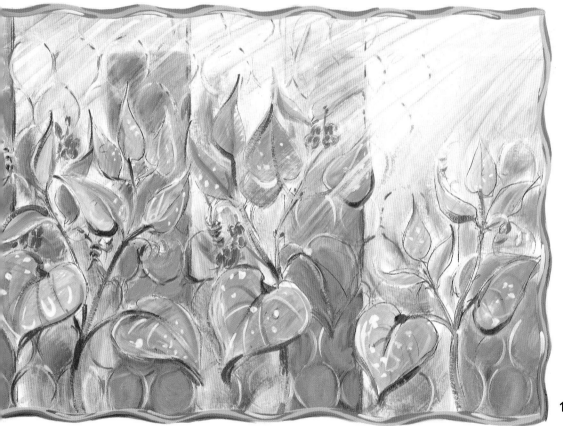

The beans liked the water
and they liked the sun.
They grew and grew.

"Look down here, Sally," said Mom.
"Look at this!
See the little green beans."

Sally took care of the beans, day after day.

"Here is a big bean," she said.
"This is a big bean, too.
Look at my beans, Mom."

"I like beans," said Sally.